SELF-PORTRAIT WITH AN UNWILLING LANDSCAPE

Laurie Blauner

Owl Creek Press
1620 N. 45th St.
Seattle WA 98103

ACKNOWLEDGMENTS

The author would like to thank the following magazines and their editors for previously publishing poems included in this collection:

The American Poetry Review: "Discussion of Marriage by Strangers Among Fireflies"

The Black Warrior Review: "When Marriage Isn't All It Could Be" and "A Housewife's Old-Fashioned Fire"

DeKalb Literary Arts Journal: "Memoirs of a Painter's Model, 1929"

The Montana Review: "The Astronaut Remembers Snow," "Compulsion," and "The Magician Practices in Front of a Mirror"

The Nebraska Review: "Protocol of Water"

The New Orleans Review: "What We Don't See"

The Pennsylvania Review: "Metamorphosis" (under the title: "The Flamboyance of Memory")

The Seattle Review: "Black and White," "Birds Misplaced by the Afternoon," and "Photograph of the Complexities of Desire"

The Wisconsin Review: "The Significance of Dreams"

Anthology of Magazine Verse and Yearbook of American Poetry

Thanks also to the Seattle Arts Commission for a grant that helped to complete this book.

cover painting by Jiri Maska

CONTENTS

for Rich Ives and Barbara Celli

''Now all he seemed to care about were the things that lived and died on a scale of time an ordinary human being could understand.''

--Thomas McGuane
Nobody's Angel

SELF-PORTRAIT WITH AN UNWILLING LANDSCAPE

FOR THE STARS

THE INSISTENCE OF LIGHT

In this the season of regrets
you think of the stars as distant leaves
shaken from a tree of light. In time
they spread out to take over the morning
of a companion's face as he tells you how
he crawled through the black drainage pipes of
one country to another. This is how we sleep;
the breath of the world against our cheeks.
A dream of branches holding a moon, holding
memory until it fades against light, a flower
losing each petal to the bloom
of the unknown we call time.

THE MAGICIAN PRACTICES IN FRONT OF A MIRROR

where what seems to exist actually doesn't or vice versa,
life a continual surprise, the wonder of a field
suddenly filled with snow or a star appearing

like a smile in the early evening.
His hands move like leaves in a wind,
a rabbit in a hat, birds, playing cards, and

scarves, red ghosts from his sleeve. He can't forget
himself. In the mirror, someone's dreams of illusion,
a flock of knives in the air, coins from an ear.

These are proof of magic, tricks revealing a cornerstone
of the unknown. We blindfold our hearts
to what we can't understand. This is entertainment

in the hour of moonlight and prayers. The magician
practices his art for his audience of silence,
for himself, the most critical child of them all.

PROTOCOL OF WATER

Tonight is our anniversary and wind fiddles,
making small waves, singing between branches.
Lakes give us our evening landscape, marriage
outlining a life. I am superstitious:
apple trees flare beneath the moon, furniture
changes shape in the dark, people become stars
after death. This lake is grained with insects.
Tiny flashes of light form every night
on the surface, musical notes reflected
in the blackness of sky. Fishermen weathered first,
cutting ice like isinglass into patterns, pulling fish
from the bottom as big as daydreams for their redhanded
wives. Lake water sinks in the gravity of each year,
knowing the landscape of our ordered world.

FLOWERS FOR AN UNFAITHFUL WIFE

The victrola sings tonight the way I imagine a house could.
Moonlight touches this world of bones
on our anniversary. Yesterday I watched you
throw our daughter into the air, a bird of paradise
unable to fly, catching her at the last minute.
You say you know women: They are red roses
turning only toward sunlight, closing to darkness like a knot
in the heart. Stars pile up in the tree branches,
an enormous blossom about to open
into the night. Sometimes I want to touch you again,
to feel our daughter's large hands or long nose.
Then you are gone, a ghost in a man's body.

In a dream I invented flowers, small stones of night
becoming breaths of color under the sun.
You held them in your arms; magenta, ochre, sienna,
until they faded into your shadow at darkness.
Our lives are our best lies: every morning you kiss me
goodbye, and in that kiss I hear a lover waiting,
the slap of an ocean. Yet landscapes are incidental.
It is the light that defines shape, a small hill visible
behind the moon where we held each other years ago.
Each button I undid released a petal of my shirt
until you touched me and stopped saying

No we can't do this. When another man did,
he brought me white roses, the trespass of desire,
in a world held still by the wide night.

RESTING AGAINST THE BACKBONE OF A LATE EVENING

the colors of this meadow's flowers are insignificant
except for the white blossoms of a freshly picked
moon withering to its stem. My heart alone
matters. He had walked with me here
in the hour of difficult images and children's dreams.
Since he has gone, I choose to live with animals
who know what lasts, sunlight of the next season
or the sky silently observing my memories.
He could be anywhere in this night. He dropped
a coin in cattails one sunset that he said
to forget. By afternoon it shone its circle
of silver light, a form of him easy to find.
It could happen again: the sky
is too wide, the moon creates too many
shadows. I think of him often
in a new meadow. He is everywhere
in this sultry evening and yet nowhere.

THE PHOTOGRAPHER'S GHOSTS

I capture every moment,
a whore holding her daughter in the firefly light of moon,
a dwarf cartwheeling on hills of snow. With other shadows
I could mistake a model's arm for the curve of a rose,
knowing memory is replaceable. I remember you best
in a flash of light, wife and son, sunlit in the crushed automobile.
A tiny fist held the air that today washes pears,
overflowing the chrome bowl like sleep descending
on the man at the all-night diner. In chimes,
in the language of bees, I hear your voices.
I spend my life in chiaroscuro,
a piano player suspended between white and black keys
finding a music lost to wind threading the nape of his neck.
Developing pictures of a Russian sailor seen through his mirror
and a child dressed as an angel, I see certain shadows
as lives gone by. I wish I could stop them.
I wish I could hold their lives
as steady as their pictures.

ON THE ANNIVERSARY OF YOUR DISCOVERY OF FLOWERS

stars gather hoping you'll notice their blossoms of light,
elegies of ice, shining their lack of color in the dark disguise
of sky. This marriage of color and scent contains
the details of life: the growth of the heart,
the buds open for whatever comes along, insects,
wind, weather. Lovers know the feeling, scenery you can't live
without, serenading the silence with heartbeats.
Excitement, the unfolding of the unknown petal by petal the way
stories of your ancestors tell about you. The landscape
of colors -- fuchsia, heather, indigo, lilac, violet, pink --
fills our world. From their perfume
you know their direction, a scent of moonlight
just before morning or a wind sculpting the ocean.
You find within the blooms a new life for the heart,
a perfection formed in just one season.

DISCUSSION OF MARRIAGE BY STRANGERS
AMONG FIREFLIES

The language of a party is portraits, people
dancing in the dark. Songs thread your life,
an imitation of art we could not have imagined.
Balloons reach high into the night sky. Tonight
you touched the cheek of a woman you never saw before,
different disguises, emotions. There is the forgetting
of children: In the sky the stars remind us
of a future we promised the way snow or insects
are sure to be in the air soon. Marriage is between
all people, the light between all the unknown
planets and earth. Or marriage is the fireflies
you watch with a blinking hope, the bouquet
of scar-white lilies you once threw, a syllable
among strangers. Everyone agrees that love bruises.
The shadows of evening wait on the side of your face,
away from house lights in the form of overlapping moons
against bone and skin. To touch the dark side
is to enter the complicity of dreams,
the costuming of strangers in clothes we recognize.
But they speak an unknown language.

REFLECTIONS IN A CAT'S EYE

The young see only themselves: arrangements of features,
diaries of their thoughts, prayers of pleasure.
You see the images of birds and waves of desire
and you think of justice in the order of nature,
the spider of blood that was once a mouse.
Sometimes the right thing to do is cruel,
the way we learn to abandon animals, suspicious
of that better life. We must disengage our hearts

from memory, that woman who reads
our old love letters and tells us how
our lives should have been. In the past
there were sacrifices, animals whose eyes
turned to glass: flies circled their faces
as we drank their blood. Now
we wonder if cats are able
to think about the signature of air
left by the flights of sparrows
or what they see in our eyes.

THE SHADOW OF ORDINARY HAPPINESS

follows us everywhere like a puddle of dark mud
behind our sadness, the way the sky
is the heartbeat of the ocean. They need each other,
these opposites: We learn about happiness by the small
changes in our lives. When the wind stops trying
to polish the stars until they are too small to be seen or
the rain stops its imitation of a criminal's footsteps,
we are relieved. It is always there waiting,
reminding us of silence or memory or someone
we have loved whose kisses later became our tears.
We cannot see its shape, resembling a cloud,
or the way it fits us after a long night's sleep. It enters
our lives as quietly as Spring touches the rosebushes;
sometimes we don't notice.

WHAT YOU MEAN WHEN YOU CALL MY NAME

In sleep, when the day's end fills with wolf-colored stars
and the wind voices regrets, small postcards of memory, you
no longer see the moon enter your dream like your wife. She
orchestrates the wind through a web of tree branches, a spider
hanging from a string. I am in your dream, the peasant girl
from Mexico whose face you call an apricot blossom, whose eyes
speak a language you do not know, who you took to your bed.
You betray yourself: The alphabet of moonlight
etches your skin and you think of my touch.
In the bright silence of moon
I know we cannot last.

And there is no answer. You think of two sparrows.
They call to one another after flying over the same striated clouds.
You hold onto the skeleton of your life. Sudden love is a darkness
that covers the sun rolling off to become shadows.
Today I see the sunrise reflected on the wings of flies
at my window. Soon comes a winter of silence and
old photographs. I imagine what you are doing.
I am an apprentice of relationships,
and I wonder whose name you call now.

THE ZOOKEEPER'S DAUGHTER

It's 1953 and everyone is confined by their habits,
unsubstantial as dragonfly wings between my fingers.
You feed the peacocks and think: The measuring of time
is all we are allowed. Yet everything is for me tonight,
the dank odor of monkeys, plum-colored seals rising like bruises
out of ice-blue water, cockatoos lifting their beaks
to a sky of children's balloons, bright, distant,
and moving as though they were alive.

Constellations take their places quietly in the sky. A laborer
watches two black dogs fight over a bone on his way home.
You are calling me under a spherical moon. Leopards
pacing their cages by memory are you; every night they dream
jungles of dark earth full of toucan wait for them. It is habit.
Here giraffes hang like balustrades in the water-colored dark.
Dance songs from a radio move toward the antelope.
Outside, the smell of straw drifts. Tonight I cannot sleep,
thinking of geese flying over this black earth,
because of something in my heart, not between
a father and daughter or even a husband and wife
but what is in the touch of moonlight on two inseparable animals.

COMPULSION

The man's cigarette smoke spirals toward an ancestral portrait of
                                                                his
grandmother as he paces the mahogany floor in my painting.
                                                          Unseen
in the next room, under the pale eyelid of moon, is a window
of rust-colored stars, clothes scattered as intrusively
as morning light, a birth. The man's motions
are frozen on canvas forever, a ruby carved in intaglio,
brightness polished into perfect angles.

My mother threw the chair she was posed with at my father
leading into a marriage outlined in charcoal. Time like sunlight
changes, the meteorology of the heart. Except
for a still life, where objects take up the space
meant for people. I have recorded
features as compulsively as a spider weaves her web.
I see my husband and he stands still so long
it is as if he is composed by half light, knowing I love him for
his tint. The world becomes what I see: a girl stopping
in an apple orchard, believing she's unobserved, the details
of her life unimportant, the only reason for me to go on.

CLOUDS

Someone passed you by today
thinking how her husband left on the night of the eclipse,
taking her collection of stones carved and colored by seawater,
and how, in that moment before words when thought has gone
like a mist of morning insects, you can change anything.
That was a night of silhouettes and dreams.
Buddy swayed, 1946, sipping whiskey; his pompadour
courted the moon, his shadow measured the length of the dance
floor.
While Buddy held you, the starlight came and went.

Clouds like memory change the weather,
and in their shapes you see other times, love or war,
a hidden moon, a little boat drifting on
the white horizon of sky. Tonight dusk diffuses
into the nape of your neck the way a stone is cast
into the water. And perhaps you'll remember
the shade of a tree widening into night, stars
pinning themselves, tiny insects, to branches,
the moment that just passed you by.

THE ARCHITECT OF SNOW

Autumn evening, the birds gone, the stars are shiny leaves
in the bare tree branches: He can't see what
he doesn't look for. Perhaps in whiteness we can lose

ourselves, a new perspective, a language of winter
that falls across the earth the way light is the moon's
signature. He walks under the evergreens, thinking snow

is a sign of change, like a love
that contours its own pale landscape, words
that drop from our lips with hope

spread out in front of us.
The ingredients are all here; the open fields,
the cold, the absence of color, and time drifting down

through empty space to cover each ordinary moment with another.
All he can do is wait. The seasons return
looking different, having been aggrieved in time.

FOR THE MOON

PORTRAIT FOR THE MOON

Today I am measured,
a still life of flesh lined by memory
like the skeleton of a fish etched in stone.
Among the monotony of this world there is beauty;
a random arrangement of white geese, tiny icicles
pinned to sky, profiles formed and reformed.

I am painted on an oak chair
in mauve and sienna. My eyes are the blackbird's
I saw from the train yesterday, wings billowing
like black clouds. Below, a man walking thought
a woman with hair the color of autumn passed him by,
but if he could show her a sunrise in these fields,

a bouquet of light, she would stay. In the window my face
was a silhouette on a moving cameo. A girl,
sitting in a red parlour chair, opened
her gold locket and cried to a picture of her mother.

Tonight I meet myself in the eyes of a world
where the moon rises and falls in the window behind me
like a tired spider. The grisled dog in the corner turns,
dreaming endless plains of brown grass. Moonlight
has no desire, while my heart, that marionette of evening,
is still as the glint of stars in ice-covered trees.

SELF-PORTRAIT WITH AN UNWILLING LANDSCAPE

Snow falls to the rhythm of my heartbeats.
Snowflakes uncertain of their purpose
melt like ordinary moments lost
in memories. I look out the window
to see what disappears from my life,
the moon eclipsing bare trees someone
else remembers as the evening
of first ice. We choose our occasions;
the unraveling of the heart,
the effect of a cross-stitch of weather
on a reluctant landscape. I can change
like these seasons. Last year
I followed a trail of snow,
every footstep so forgettable that
by the afternoon, tracks gone,
I didn't know where I was. Each moment
is the alphabet of our lives.
Leaves fade and fall, invisible
against the earth. I am a part of
that change. Tonight the white light of
the moon sees everything
yet will remember nothing.

THE OCEAN AS A GOOD LUCK CHARM

The religion of sea
means more than the drowned. Clouds follow
the lead of ocean like the white fish
of sky or the pale flowers of pilgrims.
It is our belief that gives the water its importance,
the way a drifter carries a bottle
of dirt in his pants pocket. As tonight
fills with moonlight that floats
on the waves like imagination's
long boats, you know that muscle of water
will never stop the drone of its surf,
steady as breathing, no matter what we think.

BLACK AND WHITE

There are no ghosts, only the shudder
of the migration of white-winged moths against my curtains
or the movement of snow achieving its pale harmony,
a pianist's formal gloves fluttering down from a tall building
landing camouflaged on a white cement sidewalk. At night
I grow invisible, surrounded by the darkness. Someone could
mistake me for an oak tree or a dog in that equality of blackness,
my arms arching in imitation of the moon and no one sees.
As a scientist I believe in the certainty of the senses.
A shadow spreads out from my feet, a dusky pool
when I stand facing the sun. All the explanations
are part of me, the reason the moon carves its form
in the night like the initial of a sweetheart in the bark
of a tree. This is how to live, trusting the provable,
the ice of winter pushing back the night in its sureness.

THE STUDY OF SCIENCE

After each day there is certain to be another;
all the components of the afternoon lie exposed on my table
like the intestines of a frog. In the parade of time
there are discoveries, accidents as sudden as a door
opening to sunlight or the touch of an invisible spider's web.
The world is arithmetic in its bones of light,
its ceremony of flowers and ice,
the seasons. Tonight my body will navigate the city
to eat dinner with my wife. Evening to her
is a degree of darkness in each room. I wonder
how the moon rises, the eye
of some animal walking waking from sleep. I wonder
at the separate world of the body under a microscope,
or the scurrying of spiders, the movement of planets.
Every discovery reinvents our lives,
our histories. My wife disassembles herself
for children. They will outlast us.

WHAT WE DON'T SEE

could see us. From the accident of discovery we have been given
memory, the same way we could always find our favorite toy
in the bedroom strange with darkness.
There is so much between us and understanding: the imposter
of ourselves, feelings weathered to match our ideas
of who we are, and habit, the comfort of the rain
of footsteps you hear down the hall every day, the same time
and place. What we don't see, we may never know.
And never miss the scarf of wind wrapped around
a pine or the tributary of bones in a sculptor's model
who could change your life.

THE DREAMS OF SMALL ANIMALS

flutter like the wings of tiny insects against a window
on an enormous landscape of bird-shaped clouds
and ocean-green grass. During the day there are
particular pleasures; familiar territory, a warm touch,
following your own shadow, the form of your absence.
You sift through small dreams like the bright confetti.
Your breath is soft against fur.
The silhouette of a maple tree brushes
the grass, becoming animal tracks.
You follow the tracks under the tinny sky,
paws fitting perfectly as the sharp maple leaves
in the refractable air. This is the dream,
where you find the large painting of your world,
wishbone trees on an expanse of earth
with you in the middle. You learn about the wind,
the beating of sparrow wings in an empty house,
and the moon, that habit of dreams,
before you awaken into this world.

THE SIGNIFICANCE OF DREAMS

These are the dreams you remember in waking, shadows
you've turned to catch following you as closely as the silence
pinned to your blouse, a corsage, when you walk alone.
Sometimes I feel like the wind turning a maple leaf skyward
on a tree to show its beauty or the seesaw flight
of swallows as though they were the last brown useless
leaves of autumn. Your neighbor's daughter awoke last night
crying because of a dream her body heat left waves
in the wood of her favorite chair. Her mother
scorched her hand on the girl's ribcage,
a small fire within. In the morning she had a fever
and went to the hospital. I can change your life
like the moon moving serenely across the night sky,
unaware how it makes the ocean roll.

THE FIRE-EATER WRITES HIS MOTHER

about the love for a woman that consumes his body,
a moth so close to light that its pale wings
are warm to the touch. It is nothing like eating fire,
where what is burned is gone. There is wonder in fire;
it flares and is dampened by the body that devours our lives.
Sometimes we wish our feelings belonged to a stranger.

Strangers become lovers, lips touching lips scorched
by the history of childhood. He writes that
the moon is turning everything
silver at night. You do what you didn't think
you could. He wears a piece of her hair
braided around his finger for luck, for
memory, a part of her that can't be explained.

PHOTOGRAPH: THE COMPLEXITIES OF DESIRE

My smile is that detail of moon curved
on the sky, an auspicious sign
to my father. He looks straight ahead
as though he could see the secrets
of the photographer, the bones of a cat
snow-white in his attic, a man's wife
he could never tell anyone about. My sister
gazes up at the thin puddle of clouds knowing
all our dreams by heart. There is one
about flying as a heron toward
the moon, one of a criminal who
breaks into sleeping houses, and one about
the touch of spiders on your legs at night.
We want so much to teach someone about
 the difference: pigeons and snow and
 have them want you forever.
Without desire we are left with
a black and white picture, everyone posed,
a family for the photographer who's thinking
of another man's wife. In my dreams
as in the snapshot: birds circle but never
reach the brightness of the abstract moon.

AT THE MUSEUM OF THE ORDINARY

I spotted you across the dark room studying stars
through glass. I passed by the flowers and bones,
in my dress the color of summer grass, thinking
of other people's secrets as sunlight that comes out
eventually the way you can find your favorite riverbend
a few days after it snows. I learned what arrangements
you liked: a centerpiece of trees and unmoving animals,
rows of clear stones broken in pieces glittering like
your memory of love, possibilities in the dark.
There are no seasons here, sunrise lives in the imagination,
and you've forgotten the real moon in this air.
All the strange places and towns
blossom in your heart, opening up to look like
the hidden grooves of a seashell cut in half.
Look at the past, the interiors of animals you've never
known, how we accept weather and learn to say
goodbye. I see the rows of windows are someone
ordinary's house, someone who can live with desire
fluttering by, an exhibit of birds, or night returning
the house to a blackness they lose themselves to
each evening. This is the bravery of love, entering
a corner unlit by a light we know by heart,
holding a fossil the color of ancient bones, untouched
by anyone for years, not knowing if it's real.

THE BALLERINA WHO LOST A SHOE

on the Monday afternoon war was declared, couldn't
be in her next performance, but thought of the lost slipper

as a white cat leaping into its own life in an alley somewhere or a
small pale scarf dancing in the arms of the wind, the new
                                                    possessor.

Her lover, with his fear of spiders, dreams of boats adrift and
gently pushed by lake water. She thinks he is graceful. He walks

on the Chicago street, his heartbeat
hidden in the music of his shoes.

At dawn the sonata of sunlight
begins, each tree leaf turning

to pass the glitter. He brings
red dancing slippers, the color of roses.

The shoemaker described consolation as a scar of light
resting in your hands. Silently it disappears.

MELANCHOLY ACTRESS

Moonlight fails me again this morning,
weak as a character lost in a bad play.
Sleep is the fly I want,
tossing against the window of a honey-warm June.
My leading man said *love* too many times last night.
Each rehearsal I smile at the same jokes.
Words whisper back from my palmetto.
At dinner my face is pale in the white plates.
The polished silverware suggests
something missing. I no longer feel
the recurring touch of the last actor,
leaves brushing a tree entering the heart of a wind.
I lie down in grass. Shadows cover me;
sunlight's difficult soliloquy weakens.

THE TROUBLE IS

for my mother

Each time you touch me there are no promises
of landscapes or animals. Only the rosettes of stars
clustered against a shoulder of evening know
your name. I never asked. These procedures of love
are nightly repetitions of day, where I am
Jack's wife, laying out the moons of plates
in their eternal silence. I've heard that everything
has its place: This city full of songs of dangerous
men or the woman I am as sunlight
touches our balcony the same way a prisoner
maps out a cell. Tonight the city's ritual
of lamps begins like a cigarette passed from
each man to his woman. And I wish I was
smoke, leaving the body's risky needs to search
for the quiet scar of a moon, white and faithful
in the sky. But I pray for romance, that
illusory scene of infidelity where there is nothing to lose
but yourself. I arrange glass animals stained
by light from the fireplace below, their hearts
clear, invisible, too small to see.

THE GHOSTS OF BIRDS

are clouds across the moon, are small signs of faith
in unknown territory, are mistaken for moths

in the flesh-colored light of dawn. Yesterday my father saw one
from his deathbed. Tonight moonlight rests on my shoulder

resembling the touch of a sympathetic hand.
The absence of sunlight surrounds me.

In the house I see my husband reading
my father's book. He walks in circles around the light,

a moth, wondering if grief is unable to fly.
I see comfort in this, shadows of our lives,

rising almost invisible against the ice of a lake.

SOMETIMES DESTINY

is a strand from a spider's web, the forfeiture
of light one summer evening or leaves turning in rain
like pages from a book you've read. We can't
know everything, your daughter all dressed up
with nowhere to go. Her hat, dress and shoes
are your size, one definition of style to grow into.

*

One July night you drive to your field to see
the alphabet of stars you've taught your daughter,
Orion, Andromeda. You remember your grandmother's eyes,
swallows frozen in a circle of wheat-colored ground,
in the evening light sent down from stars long cold.
You think of the stars as children who've tried to wait
up for you, falling asleep as you reach the door.

*

You've lived your death ten different ways and
haven't yet learned it. There is the art
of waves, the way the past
is spread open, the way our hearts uncurl,
waiting to be looked at like the flattened pages
of a favorite book or a spider's web
bent by the wind, unsure what to do with the gift.

FOR THE LAND

THE REFUGEE

Inez, you are a monument to something forgotten or
nothing remembered, like the stopping of a heart
arbitrarily, a leaf falling that you don't see land.
From your window you see street after street
of windows. This is a country of losses
that die with you and houses that flash into darkness
like stars, suffused with an early light and
another language. You find yourself repeating
words without meaning, until the vowels
feel right, like the moon webbed with clouds
from your childhood. A sunset the color of
Monarch butterfly wings is a small consolation
in Guatemala where your family was shot. Tonight
your breath rises to that moon, elusive as a spider,
a circular border with land you will never touch,
night walking across that delineation of new dreams
and cruelties, unfolding like a fist held tight
with all you own. Translated into this new country,
people are the landscape, mullioned between streets
and buzzing like insects over a lake. Each
has their own story, a tiny death of the heart,
a blossoming of memory called a souvenir
or a home.

THE CONFESSIONS OF THE WHITE ROSES

Never having taken the risks in our short lives
that crimson roses have, our stems bend,
petals crumbling like paper in the afternoon light.
In the arrangement of layers of evening clothes
the color scarlet is the softest accordian music, wine
the shade of an aged heart, all our wishes and dreams.
We never acted on impulse, didn't grow up
the red of cardinals or summer sunsets, buds
opening like small animal mouths. Imitating
the world around us we are silent,
white as the farthest reaches of a seashell,
untouchable as a moment of sunlight on an arm.
We are posed near the window like an artist's
model, randomness carefully arranged,
an invitation to ordered chaos.
Beauty lasts several evenings,
shadows moving deeper into sleep.
A flush can rise to our necks but
we never let it show.
Our perfume can smell like the change
of seasons or the breath of a bird,
flooding the senses, the quiet chaos of our color.

EVEN ROMANCE IN A SMALL COUNTRY

is political: The solace of your lover's body,
that border of skin, is too bourgeois for you.

In the morning you watch him
leave for an ocean you haven't seen yet.

We travel with our own ideas,
trying on new ones like exotic hats, the way

music, in another language, is a kindness.
We compare pasts, myths, suspicions, entertainments.

And you think of the country's body, a dance,
an echoing syllable under the same sky you left.

Tourists believe in differences,
the meaning in the touch of a new friend,

a horizon in the bruise of evening,
the ring of bullets

meant for someone you have just met,
could have loved for several days.

IN STORIES OF DANGER

1.
The language of rain follows your children
to school, a neighborhood stranger murmuring

of storms or far away places where umbrellas
are unnecessary. Between each small breath,

footsteps loud as weather, desperate as
passionate kisses. The words become music.

Fear keeps the children from dancing, keeps
the wind from entering another country.

2.
The familiar is absent or unnoticed the way
you cannot look at the room or the victim

but only the killer's face in the movies.
Imagine him petting your cat to abstraction

in the brutal air like the only dancer
who didn't realize the song had ended. There is

always hope, seeing your reflection
in his eyes until he is no longer visible.

3.
The detective scorns an ordinary life,
the dull wife, plain house, possibility of children.

Think of expectations as constant
waves landing on the sun-bleached shore.

He follows shadows deep in
the moonless night. Fear is an apple

dropping in a windy orchard.

THE FORTUNE TELLER'S CHILD

doesn't know what to do with her hands.
They flutter like sailboats in the middle
of a sea storm. They are flat
and hidden as a shore.

She knows what the palms reveal, a future
for someone else, for the visitor
landscaped with fake jewelry who no longer lives
in the ordinary world.

Is she the child of ghosts, those birds
of the heart that come and go like the rain?
The visitors don't enjoy change.
Wanting to kiss her mother she thinks

she will fade away, a moon moving into dawn
or a hat lost in the wind. And she knows
her mother doesn't think about her much
with her stones as playmates, sunlight as music,

and dreams of an ocean she has never seen.

BIRDS MISPLACED BY THE AFTERNOON

don't realize they've grown older, time passing through them,
brushing their feathers like an evening wind or the way I become
slower, the motion of the moon away from stars toward the
                                                    morning.
I lose memories, my husband still as a tattoo against a rainy
vacation landscape the color of glass angels, the fragile catechism
of sex we returned to again and again, the children's
invitations on Sunday afternoons.

The heart is a tree full of sparrows left empty
on the first day of winter. I dreamt I was a woman
who worked in a cabaret, listening to men's breath rising
and falling like a dance, laughter furring my skin like silk.
In my dreams of youth there were no pleasures, not the aged touch
of bone on curved bone, two etched shells washed from an ocean,

still tangled. Time reminds me that we are misplaced
by people we've known, like strays waiting for the recognizable,
full of love for companions who've given up on us.
Birds don't show age the way we do, the syncopation
of ice in the bourbon no longer allowed, melodies growing softer,
full of the sadness from the nightly winds of childhood.

ALCHEMY OF THE HEART

This tropical afternoon history goes on without you:
Dragonflies and ordinary marriages stain the windows
like beads of water on a cold glass. You see the scar on your arm
reflected on the pane as a thin moon etched on your child's body,
rising and falling, or a cat's white whisker against an elbow of
heat. You watch your mother outside bring your father lemonade,
a Chinese fan painted with a yellow dragon surrounded by a red
sea of fire. He has lost his job and your mother thinks of how
the movements of the butterflies should delight him,
the way water glides over rocks in a stream.
But your father sees only a cloud of insects whose wings
are a confusion of colors, the round shadow
under each white blossom of the apple tree.

THE LANDSCAPE REARRANGED WITH ICE OR FLOWERS

is in our dreams of seasons that the clouds ignore,
is part of a bird's world where there are no shadows,
only a darkness that holds everything. It happens
in one night, the way we lose ourselves each evening,
closing our eyes to fear, noise, children. When we awaken
there is an ice that seems to reproach us
for our failures, saying we cannot touch but only
skate over them. The woods are glass-colored.
The hills look carved out of rain. In the face
of the curious moon we see the cool distance
of memories, wishing they could be changed. The stars
are frozen in the sky. One day there are flowers
flaring up on the hills to remind us of the beauty
of our pasts, the rosebush spreading like a sunset
from last summer or jonquils lifted by wind
like a sonata played by the blind musician.
The woods are full of color, an ocean. At night
stars are small silver buds in a black mirror.
We try to remember winter, its own language
drifting through us to touch the earth.

BELIEVING THE EARTH FLAT

for Ruth Beskin

Rain washes the moon: Light falls
on an empty glass and velvet sofa, a mistake.
The world is what it appears to be:
random. Even in our dreams there is the understanding

that anything can happen, years cease
to follow one another. The curves of our bones
rearrange themselves into animal shapes.
In this landscape of winter moonlight and

edges we see all
we know. To learn about the language of colors
in a grove of aspen, fish from the silence of
mirrors, sorrow from a girl weeping,

do we give up ideas
for love, where one likes roundness and one flatness,
discovering belief?

A HISTORY OF SPIDERS

At first we thought they weaved
        the sky
with its glittery geometry -- the moon descending,
        a white spider.

Trees rise, dark insects
        caught
in the cocoon of night. This is the history
        of our thought,

where you've watched a man describe
        a woman
by tracing his hands through the air
        or a kiss

sent through the glass window
        at a party,
an attempt at making something
        out of nothing.

Their touch is as soft and silent
        as smoke
and you wonder what they think of
        the ladder of skin

on your arms and legs. Resembling
        a stain
or a bruise, they exist in the corners
        of our lives,

entering our day by the smallest string,
        like a woman
unfolding worn lace to find a letter, a memory
        she doesn't open.

METAMORPHOSIS

The end of each season is a collapse:
ants climbing a trail of maple frozen like beads of water on a glass,
the first bee wedged in a rose's heart,
fundamentals of time. From the hospital window,
a gray cat in an old-fashioned chase with a yellow leaf,
the red vengeance of sunrise, my wife sitting
by the whisper of a fire. Death comes too quickly.
Leukemia lacquers my body, a ritual
leaving me dependent on my mind. My thoughts deceive
the boy, a tourniquet, winter's snowfall
gently covers the debris of autumn.
At the Bikini test in 1946 we watched the earth split
into a new shape, a pebble cast into the lake of ground.
No moment is as bright. I watch car headlights return
to the homes of ordinary lives.

MEMOIRS OF A PAINTER'S MODEL, 1929

I am as important as landscape to you,
the kaleidoscope of light through clouds
or the revision of wildflowers by sunset each night.
I once thought you prized a horse the color of earth more
until he would not stay still for you.

I have learned the architecture of my body
like a prayer reshaped every evening
to fulfill our desires. You use a romantic's, a mapmaker's
language to pose me. "Move your head to the east
as if to watch the moon seed the sky with stars."

For you I ignore time, that learning by heart of
boundries, a shadow interrupted by light.
Why must I hold the same position day after day?
You want to recapture what is already lost
like a dancer practicing the same steps

for another performance. Those abstract figures
on the canvas do not look like me, perhaps
a dream of me in pale colors, a faded
stained glass window. You kissed my soft angles once
in a painting as though they could kiss you back

like a child's puppet on a hand. You see me
in the colors of birds and the light of saints,
not needing to apologize to memory, that arrangement of
                                                    moments.
But you never understand when I am finished posing
how the life I return to is changed again
and still outside your life.

THREE USES OF MEMORY

1. The Music Box Collector

To begin the evening again with the regalia of each song,
notes rising like mist or ghosts toward a chandelier of stars,
in tune with the stammering wind of winter. It has happened
                                                    before
as a boy when you leaned against every moment, your mother's
lullabies in the darkening sky, tiny feather closing on
themselves, until you too floated into empty space like smoke
or clear sound, thinking of nothing. The family photographs
in tangerine frames on the fireplace want
to hear the silence. Open the boxes, a flash of birds,
the tapping of stars against the windows like
frozen insects or the kisses of a very young girl.
Music has no past. Melody enters the light
of a moon behind bronchial tree branches.
When the girl winks it is only you.

2. A Housewife's Old-Fashioned Fire

Not so much the faces, eyebrows askew, lipstick smeared as
though
applied at dusk without a mirror, the expressions of animals
you forgot but once knew by name, not so much the monotony of
light
carved on furniture day after day, but the company you keep.
A flame-colored cockatoo sings of life from its tall cage,
its songs blending the light from a full, orange moon,
the shadows of different trees. In every blade of fire
you hope for more. One night, just fifteen, you turned
your lips red against the grass in summer moonlight. The barn
at the end of the meadow lit your lipstick and in its next life
you saw changing boundries, constellations' light
reshaping your features, a new kind of make-up, eyelids
florid as roses pressing against glass for release. In the fire
is the face you saw in the shop window yesterday,
small and dark as a piece of burnt paper in a landscape.

3. Sadness

Unchanging, the lake I know is green even in
the shadow-colored darkness; he stands under the ice.
A frozen scarecrow with an old hat etched by the veins of ice,
he is skeletal in my husband's clothes,
a wishbone ceremoniously left by a neighbor's dog.
He is a scarf stolen from someone's neck by the wind, left flat
and empty, the rustling of old, dry corn his lullaby,
a companion in the astronomy of the heart. I borrowed
my daughter's nightmare: a swarm of locusts
covered the farm and I crushed the small bodies
against the wall, a tapestry of grisly boutonnieres.
Light from constellations invades the house tonight, settling
like a blossom of gnats on the photograph of my husband.
His heart stopped last year in the field. The moon
is not a crooked smile of light, the top
of a wave, but only a fixture in the bruised sky.

MY GOOD YEARS

are etched on the ice among the hairline cracks,
lines crossed so many times there are no ends or beginnings.
It snows today, promises forgotten under the whiteness.
The body is a bad romance, a betrayal of what you know
 so well, a love that reaches perfection only to disassemble,
like the seasons. There was a time
when I could dance on ice, a child under
the winter moon whose face resembled my mother's.
The wind passed through bare branches. I could turn
and jump like that wind on ice so thin
it was music, suspending me between this life
and another. What makes our past
remain in one form or another? Winter,
a season that is part of the world that breaks
away from you, a wind, while you remain.

WHEN MARRIAGE ISN'T ALL IT COULD BE

you think of the red leaves
of a beauty's lips blossoming on white napkins
in the mansion of the stories from your childhood.
What would she do, after leaving the imprint
of a crimson apple cut in two halves,
a broken heart on the table, her mark?
Either leave before sunrise in a long dark cape
embroidered with a silver star for a life
of adventure or stay in the old Victorian house
wondering where the evening stars are swept to
by the wind before morning. It is a gilded bird
that calls her from sleep's dreams like a husband.
When it rains he unbuttons her blouse,
the way we climb down a ladder or
sketch a nude in abstract lines,
until the piece of silk falls to the floor.
She becomes a statue the sculptor calls
out of clay, red rose of a mouth against
her body, arms fluttering graceful as pigeons.
Her eyebrows are crescent moons, a representation
of who she really is. She thinks of all she is owed.

THE ASTRONAUT REMEMBERS SNOW

The sky is my world, one foot after another in air.
There is a light from someone else's past, a memory like a name
mentioned long ago and memory is the choosing of a moment
from all the ones gone by, a meteor grazing metal.
I remember the touch of my dying mother,
weightless on my arm and then damp on my skin.
I caught those pieces of the stars on my tongue in winter,
last words passed from mouth to mouth. And I miss
what I've known so well, what I'll return to --
history, time made important, ice against a window,
or flowers that blossom into events. There is so much space, so
                                        much silence,
her face upturned, beautiful, white under her last blue sky.

THE MOON'S SENSE OF DIRECTION

The small boy arranges his shadow in the heart of a tree
with the assurance of a sparrow. Tonight the moon
will perch in the bones of the trees
to watch him. It happens every night,
the way his parents tell him stories. Memory lives

in the breath of world.
Rain falls into the dreams of animals.
He has never seen the moon
hesitate on its path through the evening sky.
His diary of seasons continues,

predicting the movement of clouds,
the first snow. He has become an observer,
with the patience of a blossoming jonquil, watching the world
relive time with its small changes.
He thinks of leaves on a tree.

OBSESSIONS

How do you forget about snow in the middle
        of winter
when the only movement is a heron's shadow

swimming the ice of a river, when
        the hills
resemble the snowfield

of your shirt, white-sheeted furniture from
        an old summer house?
Watch snow argue with the wind,

form its own landscape, cover its mistakes
        like a couple
together so long through the bad seasons

they know all the flaws and curves of
        each other's bodies.
The shape of every day has no words,

just the habit of a wife cutting
        an apple open
to carve out the white fruit

that her husband likes best. Try to think
        of something else;
what forms in the crevices of our lives,

the small dreams that stick,
        an ice we can see better.
Look forward to the ordinary,

a first snowfall, the path
        of a moonlit river,
an evening walk.

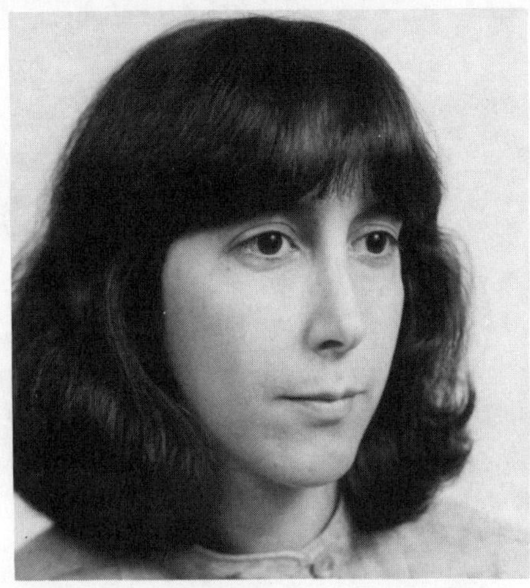

Laurie Blauner was born in 1953, raised in New York City, and educated at Kenyon College, Sarah Lawrence College and the University of Montana where she received an MFA in Creative Writing in 1980. Her poems have been published in *American Poetry Review*, *The Georgia Review*, *Poetry*, *Poetry Northwest* and numerous other magazines. She currently lives and works in Seattle and received a Seattle Arts Commission Writing Award in 1988.